Here Is the Wetland

Madeleine Dunphy

ILLUSTRATED BY

Wayne McLoughlin

Web of Life
CHILDREN'S BOOKS

H
ere is the wetland.

Here is the water
both shallow and still
that soaks the soil
of this murky, moist world:
Here is the wetland.

Here are the cattails
that grow in the water
both shallow and still
that soaks the soil
of this murky, moist world:
Here is the wetland.

Here is the muskrat
that eats the cattails
that grow in the water
both shallow and still
that soaks the soil
of this murky, moist world:
Here is the wetland.

Here is the mink
who hunts the muskrat
that eats the cattails
that grow in the water
both shallow and still
that soaks the soil
of this murky, moist world:
Here is the wetland.

Here are the bass
that swim from the mink
who hunts the muskrat
that eats the cattails
that grow in the water
both shallow and still
that soaks the soil
of this murky, moist world:
Here is the wetland.

Here is the heron
which stalks the bass
that swim from the mink
who hunts the muskrat
that eats the cattails
that grow in the water
both shallow and still
that soaks the soil
of this murky, moist world:
Here is the wetland.

Here is the frog
that leaps from the heron
which stalks the bass
that swim from the mink
who hunts the muskrat
that eats the cattails
that grow in the water
both shallow and still
that soaks the soil
of this murky, moist world:
Here is the wetland.

Here is the snake

who preys on the frog

that leaps from the heron

which stalks the bass

that swim from the mink

who hunts the muskrat

that eats the cattails

that grow in the water

both shallow and still

that soaks the soil

of this murky, moist world:

Here is the wetland.

Here are the blackbirds

that wing past the snake

who preys on the frog

that leaps from the heron

which stalks the bass

that swim from the mink

who hunts the muskrat

that eats the cattails

that grow in the water

both shallow and still

that soaks the soil

of this murky, moist world:

Here is the wetland.

Here are the bulrushes
that hold up the blackbirds

that wing past the snake

who preys on the frog

that leaps from the heron

which stalks the bass

that swim from the mink

who hunts the muskrat

that eats the cattails

that grow in the water

both shallow and still

that soaks the soil

of this murky, moist world:

Here is the wetland.

*H*ere are the coots
that hide in the bulrushes
that hold up the blackbirds
that wing past the snake
who preys on the frog
that leaps from the heron
which stalks the bass
that swim from the mink
who hunts the muskrat
that eats the cattails
that grow in the water
both shallow and still
that soaks the soil
of this murky, moist world:
Here is the wetland.

*H*ere are the ducks
who live near the coots
that hide in the bulrushes
that hold up the blackbirds
that wing past the snake
who preys on the frog
that leaps from the heron
which stalks the bass
that swim from the mink
who hunts the muskrat
that eats the cattails
that grow in the water
both shallow and still
that soaks the soil
of this murky, moist world:
Here is the wetland.

Here is the water
that is home to the ducks
who live near the coots
that hide in the bulrushes
that hold up the blackbirds
that wing past the snake
who preys on the frog
that leaps from the heron
which stalks the bass
that swim from the mink
who hunts the muskrat
that eats the cattails
that grow in the water
both shallow and still
that soaks the soil
of this murky, moist world:
Here is the wetland.

Wildlife of the Wetland

MALLARD

GREAT BLUE HERON

MINK

SMALLMOUTH BASS

MUSKRAT

The wetland portrayed in this book is a freshwater marsh. Freshwater marshes are the most common type of wetland in North America. Some other types of wetlands include saltwater marshes, bogs, and swamps. Some wetlands are wet all of the time while others are dry for one or more seasons a year. Wetlands are found from the tundra to the tropics and on every continent except Antarctica.

In the past, wetlands were often regarded as wastelands—sources of mosquitoes and disease. They were seen as places to avoid or better yet to eliminate. Because of this, less than half of the original wetlands in the United States still exist.

We now know that wetlands provide food and habitat for thousands of species. Millions of waterbirds depend on wetlands for survival and more than one-third of the nation's endangered species live only in wetlands. Migratory birds

AMERICAN COOT

RED-BELLIED WATER SNAKE

RED-WINGED BLACKBIRD

BULLFROG

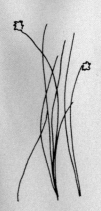

HARDSTEM BULRUSH

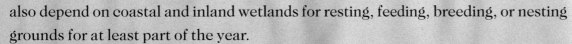

also depend on coastal and inland wetlands for resting, feeding, breeding, or nesting grounds for at least part of the year.

These areas are also critically important to humans. Wetlands absorb and filter pollutants that would otherwise contaminate groundwater, rivers, lakes, and estuaries. By holding water like sponges, wetlands help to control flooding and prevent soil erosion. Many of our food sources also come from wetlands.

Despite these many benefits, wetlands continue to be threatened by human activities such as farming, ranching, and the building of roads, dams, and towns. We must act now to help ensure the survival of wetlands. To find out what you can do, or to learn more about wetlands, write to Environmental Concern Inc., "All About Wetlands," P.O. Box P, St. Michaels, MD 21663 or visit their website at www.wetland.org.

For my darling daughter, Gwendolyn.
—M.D.

For my little camping friend, Allison.
—W. McL.

Text © 2007 by Madeleine Dunphy.
Illustrations © 1996 by Wayne McLoughlin.

First published in 1996 by Hyperion Books for Children.

For information, write to:
Web of Life Children's Books
P.O. Box 2726, Berkeley, California 94702

Published in the United States in 2007 by Web of Life Children's Books.

Printed in Singapore.

Library of Congress Control Number: 2006935413

ISBN 0-9773795-8-2 (paperback edition)
978-0-9773795-8-3

ISBN 0-9773795-9-0 (hardcover edition)
978-0-9773795-9-0

The artwork for this book was prepared using watercolor.

Read all the books in the series:
Here Is the African Savanna, Here Is the Tropical Rain Forest, Here Is the Arctic Winter, Here Is the Coral Reef, Here Is the Southwestern Desert, and *Here Is Antarctica.*

For more information about our books, and the authors
and artists who create them, visit our website:
www.weboflifebooks.com